# Hot Air Ballooning

by Christie Costanzo

**Published By**
**Capstone Press, Inc.**
**Mankato, Minnesota USA**

Distributed By

 CHILDRENS PRESS®

CHICAGO

# CIP
## LIBRARY OF CONGRESS CATALOGING IN PUBLICATION DATA

Costanzo, Christie.
    Hot air ballooning / by Christie Costanzo.
        p. cm. – (Action sports)
    Summary: Describes the history, equipment, and techniques of hot air ballooning and examines some of its competitions and popular locations.

    ISBN 1-56065-04-4:
    1. Hot air ballooning – Juvenile literature. (1. Hot air balloons.
    2. Balloons.) I. Title. II. Series.
    TL638.C67    1989
    629.133'22 – dc20                                  89-38673
                                                            CIP
                                                            AC

## PHOTO CREDITS

The Balloon Works, Inc.: 4, 7, 9, 11, 12, 18, 21, 22, 25,
                                    26, 28, 32, 36, 38, 42, 47, 48
World Balloon Corporation: 46

Copyright ©1991 by Capstone Press, Inc. All rights reserved. No part of this book may be reproduced in any form without written permission from the publisher, except for brief passages included in a review. Printed in the United States of America.

## CAPSTONE PRESS
Box 669, Mankato, MN 56001

EAD LIBRARY
HEBOYGAN, WISCONSIN

9000702341

702341

# Contents

A Flight in a Hot Air Balloon ................ 5

The History of Hot Air Ballooning ......... 10

How Does a Hot Air
Balloon Work? .................................... 19

Equipment Needed for
Hot Air Ballooning ............................ 23

Preparing the Balloon for Lift Off ......... 29

The Job of the Ground Crew .............. 33

Races, Rallies and Competitions
for Hot Air Balloons ............................ 39

How to get Involved in
Hot Air Ballooning ............................ 43

# A Flight in a Hot Air Balloon

It is early morning. The sun has just risen over the distant mountains. A purple, pink, and yellow hot air balloon sits quietly in the middle of a grassy meadow, waiting to fly. The wicker basket is being held in place by five members of the ground crew. The pilot makes a final check of his equipment. Everything is ready.

With a twist of the valve on the propane burner, the pilot sends a blast of fire up into the balloon. The noise from the burner sounds like the roar of a dragon. The flames heat the air trapped in the balloon and the giant bag of hot air strains upward.

"Hands off!" the pilot orders. The ground crew releases the balloon and steps back. Slowly, without a sound, the balloon rises into the clear, blue sky.

The pilot turns the valve on the burner again shooting another blue flame up into the balloon. The colorful bag of hot air rises higher in the sky. For the pilot and his two passengers there is no feeling of motion. As they climb higher and higher the passengers look down at the ground.

Everything seems to be shrinking. The ground crew look like small bugs and the chase vehicle looks like a toy car. The ground seems to be slipping away. As they climb higher, the trees begin to look like tiny bushes and nearby houses look like the game pieces on a Monopoly board.

Except for an occasional blast from the burner, the flight is silent. Because the balloon travels with the wind and not through it, there is not even the sound of moving air. The call of a crow is heard. Looking down, the balloonists see two crows flying below them. "We are higher than the birds," a passenger exclaims. And still they climb higher.

Down on the ground, the chase vehicle bounces over a dirt road trying to keep up with the balloon. The ground crew must always keep their balloon in sight. They need to be there when the balloon finally lands. Sometimes the ground crew loses sight of the balloon or cannot get to where the balloon has landed. Then the pilot and passengers must land the balloon by themselves. This can be difficult and sometimes dangerous.

Floating like a cloud, the balloon drifts over a neighborhood. A dog barks at the strange shape moving silently across the sky. Beyond the houses the pilot spots a big park.

"That looks like a good place to land," says the pilot. "We will aim for the middle of the baseball field."

The park will make an excellent landing site. There are only a few tall trees and no power lines. The streets around the park make it easy for the chase team to meet the balloon. Children who were playing on the jungle gym begin pointing at the sky. "Look! It's a balloon!" When they see it's going to land in the park, they climb off the play equipment and start running after the balloon.

The ground crew arrives first and keeps the children back and out of danger. The pilot has let the air in the balloon cool down. The balloon begins to drop. Once over the park, the pilot pulls down on the maneuvering vent rope. This opens a small hole in the side of the balloon so hot air will escape. This will make the balloon fall a little faster.

The balloon is now within one hundred feet of the ground. One of the passengers drops the towline over the side of the basket. The ground crew will grab hold of the towline to hold the balloon in place when the balloon lands. The pilot shuts off the burner. "Get ready. We're going to land." The passengers brace themselves.

Just as the basket hits the grass, the pilot pulls down hard on the ripcord. This opens a large hole at the top of the balloon. Hot air quickly escapes through the hole. This keeps the balloon from taking off again.

As the balloon begins to collapse, the ground crew scrambles to grab the side lines. One crew member finds the crown line. This is the rope attached to the top of the balloon. By pulling hard on this line, he pulls the collapsing balloon over on its side. Now the wind cannot pull the balloon away.

With all the lines held firmly in place, the pilot and passengers can leave the basket. The balloonists and ground crew exchange hugs, handshakes, and congratulations. It was a perfect flight!

# The History of Hot Air Ballooning

Hot air ballooning was invented in the kitchen. Joseph and Etiene Montgolfier discovered that they could float paper bags of hot air over their kitchen fire. Later they built a larger air bag made of fabric and paper. They hung a small cage under their balloon.

At Versailles, France in front of King Louis XVI, the first hot air balloon took to the sky. But the passengers were not people. The Montgolfier brothers sent a duck, a rooster, and a lamb up in their balloon.

Two months later, on November 21, 1783, the Montgolfiers launched another balloon. This time the passengers were human. Pilatre de Rozier and The Marquis d'Arlandes became the first aeronauts. An aeronaut is a balloon pilot.

Another Frenchman, Jacques Charles, was also interested in balloons. He filled his balloons with a gas that was lighter than air. The gas is called hydrogen. One of his first balloons climbed to 3,000 feet. When a rainstorm brought the balloon down in a small village the peasants were frightened. They thought the balloon was a giant monster. Using pitch forks and clubs they ripped the fabric air bag into shreds. Later that same year, Jacques Charles and Noel Robert flew in a gas-filled balloon. The flight lasted two hours. They traveled 25 miles and landed safely in a field outside the city of Paris.

By 1800, two types of balloons were in use, hot air and gas filled. Hot air balloons were called "Montgolfiers," to honor the famous brothers. Gas-filled balloons were called "Charliers," named after Jacques Charles. Even today these two names are used to describe the two different kinds of balloons.

Because it was hard to carry enough fuel to keep hot air balloons airborne, most of the record-setting flights took place in gas-filled balloons. The first flight across the English Channel took place in a Charlier. Jean-Pierre Blanchard and Dr. John Jeffries were the brave passengers. At first, the balloon sailed happily above the ocean. Suddenly the balloon began to drop. If they hit the water they would sink! After Blanchard threw out all the extra weight, the balloon slowly began to rise again. They finally made it across the Channel without getting wet.

The first balloon to fly in the United States carried a 13-year-old boy high above the city of Baltimore in 1784. This balloon did not fly free but was held in place with long ropes called **tethers.** The first man to fly without tethers in the United States was the Frenchman Blanchard. He flew over the city of Philadelphia while President George Washington watched from below.

In the beginning, the main purpose of hot air ballooning was to see how high or how far a person could travel. One year after Blanchard's flight over Philadelphia, the French government organized the world's first Balloon Corps. Balloons were going to war.

Balloons helped Napoleon win the battle at Fleurus by allowing his soldiers to spy on the enemy. The balloons were held in place with tethers while the crew watched troop movements from high in the sky. Tethered balloons were also used during the Civil War. A telegraph line ran from the balloon to the ground. The balloon crew could send messages to soldiers on the ground, telling them where the enemy was moving. With the invention of airplanes, balloons were seldom used for war again.

One of the greatest balloon voyages ever made began in St. Louis, Missouri on July 2, 1859. John Wise, an American balloonist, believed there was a great river of air which flowed from the west to the east. He believed that a balloonist could find this air current and could sail across the Atlantic Ocean. Everyone thought he was crazy. Finally a wealthy businessman agreed to pay for a test flight. Wise would try to fly his balloon, the "Atlantic", from St. Louis, Missouri to New York City.

John Wise and three other men rose into the sky over St. Louis to the cheers of the crowd. They drifted over farmland and cities, always moving east. They passed silently over Lake Erie and Niagara falls. Then they were hit by a violent storm which sent them crashing into the trees. Luckily no one was hurt.

John Wise piloted his balloon almost 1,000 miles from St. Louis to Henderson, New York in nineteen hours.

The "Atlantic" held the record for the longest balloon trip made in America, until 1910.

One hundred and nineteen years after John Wise's historic flight, three men from Albuquerque, New Mexico did what John Wise could not. They flew across the Atlantic Ocean in a helium-filled balloon. The year was 1978. Ben Abruzzo, Maxie Anderson and Larry Newman guided the Double Eagle II from Presque Isle, Maine to Miserey, France. They were in the air for 137 hours and traveled 3,120 miles in their boat-shaped gondola. A gondola is another name for the balloon basket.

Two years later, Maxie Anderson and his son Kris flew their helium-filled balloon, the "Kitty Hawk", across America. They started their trip at Fort Baker, California. They traveled 2,417 miles to the Gaspe Peninsula, near Matane, in Canada. The father and son team became the first balloonists to cross the continent, non-stop, in a balloon.

The Andersons were the first to fly from coast to coast. But they landed 160 miles short of the ocean. The record for flying from ocean to ocean was set in October of 1981 by John

Shoecraft and Fredrick Gorrell. In their balloon, "The Super Chicken III", they flew from the Pacific Ocean to the Atlantic Ocean in two days, seven hours and 25 minutes. This was a new record.

As of 1980, a balloon had never sailed over the Pacific Ocean. It was a challenge waiting to be met. The ballooning team of Ben Abruzzo, Larry Newman, Ron Clark and Rocky Aoki accepted the challenge. In 1981, traveling in the **Double Eagle V**, the four balloonists flew from Nagashima, Japan, to near Covelo, California, in less than four days. The **Double Eagle V** flew through a thunder and lightning storm. Somewhere over the Pacific Ocean, but not too far from land, the balloon began to leak. By crash landing in California, the crew made it home. The 5,070 miles covered on this trip is the farthest a balloon had ever traveled until January 17, 1991.

Two balloonists, Per Lindstrand and Richard Branson piloted their hot air balloon, "Pacific Flyer", across the ocean 6,761 miles. They took off from Miyakonojo, Japan on January 15th and landed two days later on a frozen lake 200 miles NW of the town of Yellowknife in Canada. On January 17th, Lindstrand and Branson set a new long distance record for hot air ballooning.

Have all the records been set? Not yet! There will always be new records to break for the longest flight and the highest flight. And still, no

one has yet made a successful trip around the world in a balloon. As long as the skies are clear and the wind is gentle, hot air ballooning will continue to attract men and women who want to reach new goals and establish new records.

# How Does A Hot Air Balloon Work?

Have you ever wondered what makes a balloon rise up into the air? And once you get up their, how do you get down? As the Montgolfier brothers observed over their kitchen fire, smoke and hot air rises. When air is heated, it expands. This creates more space between the molecules, making the air lighter. Hot air is lighter than cold air. When a balloon is filled with hot air, it rises. When the air inside of the balloon begins to cool, the balloon starts to drop.

Gas-filled balloons are different. They use special gases which are lighter than air. Hydrogen and helium are the two most common gases used for ballooning. The gas-filled balloon can be brought down to earth by letting some of the gas escape.

A balloon is sailing above the trees and suddenly the wind changes. Now the balloon is

heading for a mountain. How can the pilot make his balloon climb higher into the sky so he won't hit the mountain?

If the pilot is in a gas-filled balloon, he must throw something overboard. Balloonists in gas balloons carry extra weight called ballast. The ballast is thrown out to make the balloon lighter. Now it can climb higher.

If the pilot is in a hot-air balloon, he can shoot a flame into the opening of the balloon with his burner. This will heat up the air inside the balloon. The hotter the air inside the balloon, the lighter the balloon becomes and the higher it flies. The pilot must be careful not to overheat the bal-loon. This could damage the fabric and make holes at the top of the balloon.

A balloon must go where the wind takes it. The pilot cannot steer the balloon. A smart pilot studies the weather. He can tell which way the wind is blowing by watching the leaves fluttering on a tree or how a flag is waving.

There are currents of air flowing above the earth. When the pilot wants to fly to the east, he tries to find a river of air moving in that direction. Sometimes the wind closer to the ground is blowing to the east, while the wind a thousand feet above the ground is blowing to the west. Under these conditions, a clever pilot could

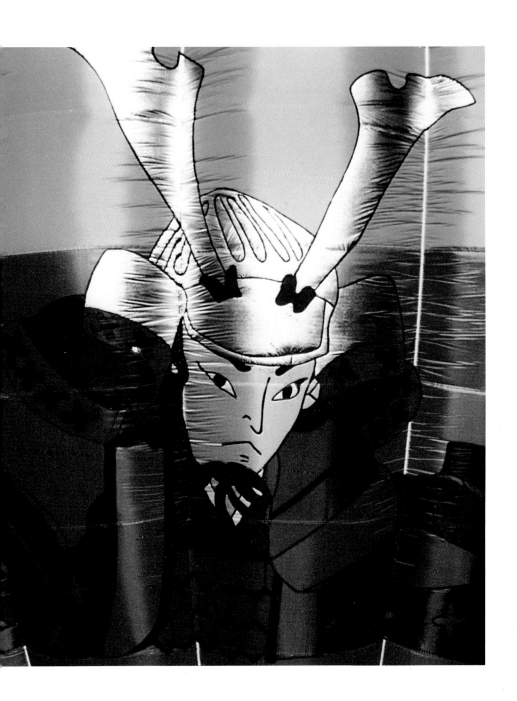

launch and land his balloon from the same area. He would fly to the east in the lower current and then come back in the upper current. This does not happen very often.

# Equipment Needed for Hot Air Ballooning

Hot air ballooning is an exciting sport. People of all ages can float like a cloud in the sky. Dalyn Miller of Carlsbad, New Mexico flew in a friend's balloon when he was two years old. By the time he was ten, Dalyn had become an active member of the ground crew. "Hot air ballooning is an experience everyone should try." says Dalyn.

Do you want to go ballooning? Here is your shopping list. The first thing you will need is the balloon, also called the envelope. This is usually made from specially treated ripstop nylon or polyester. This material is much stronger than the silk fabric used in the past. Each balloon owner creates his own design. The balloon company will sew the fabric envelope to order. This way each beautiful balloon is unique and special.

Balloons come in many different sizes and shapes. Most sport balloons stand as tall as a six story building. The bigger the balloon the more air it holds and the heavier the load it can carry. Some balloons are not balloon-shaped at all. Unusually shaped balloons can be found at festivals and rallies. Some of the strange shapes floating around the sky include castles, spaceships, prehistoric monsters and witches.

The next piece of equipment you will need is the basket, also called a gondola. The most popular basket is still made of wicker. The wicker baskets are both strong and flexible. They can be bounced along the ground by a strong wind without falling apart. The basket can also be made out of aluminum tubing or fiber-glass panels.

Check your list; balloon, basket, fuel. Without the fuel the balloon will never get off the ground. The problem with the hot air balloons of the past was the fuel system. It was difficult to carry enough fuel for a long flight. The gas-filled balloons stayed in the air longer since no fuel was carried aboard. But these balloons were expensive to fill. It cost between $2,000 and $4,000 to fill a balloon with helium. Most people could not afford to spend so much money.

Finally a solution was found. Ed Yost developed the modern hot air balloon. Yost built a balloon out of nylon and used a lightweight propane burner to heat the air in the balloon. It

costs between $20 and $30 for the propane fuel. Now ballooning was much more affordable.

In the future, balloonists may not even need fuel. Solar-powered balloons are now being tested. These balloons use the sun's rays to heat the air inside the bag. A solar-powered balloon called the "Sunstat" has already made a four hour flight above Albuquerque, New Mexico.

Before you can take to the air you will need a few instruments to insure a safe flight. A pilot will depend on three important gauges while flying. The **altimeter** measures the balloon's height above the ground. The **variometer** shows how fast a balloon is climbing or falling. The **pyrometer** tells the pilot the temperature of the air inside the balloon. These are the three main instruments a pilot needs to make a safe flight. Other equipment which is helpful includes a compass, maps, and a two-way radio to keep in contact with the chase team.

Now you are ready to load your balloon into the chase vehicle and drive out to the launching site.

# Preparing the Balloon for Liftoff

Most balloon flights occur in the early morning when the air is cool and calm. A pilot will not launch his balloon if it is raining or if the wind is too strong. A light breeze, under 10 MPH, and clear skies are the best flying conditions.

The launch area is selected with safety in mind. The site should be well away from tall trees and high powerlines. There should be plenty of room to lay out the fabric bag on a smooth surface. The ground crew checks for rocks and other sharp objects which might tear a hole in the balloon. Once the area is clear, the balloon can be rolled out.

There are special numbers marked on the balloon fabric. These numbers help the crew lay out the ballon properly. In this way they can keep the balloon's ropes from becoming twisted and tangled.

The fuel tanks are loaded into the wicker basket. The basket is tipped on its side while the burner is mounted on its bracket. Next the cables and ropes, which hold the balloon to the basket, are attached. Now the balloon is ready to be inflated.

It takes two steps to inflate the balloon. First, the balloon is filled with cold air and then the air is heated. The crew members go to their positions. One person must hold the crown line. This is the rope attached to the top of the balloon. The person holding the crown line will keep the balloon from "standing up" too soon.

Two more people are needed to hold ropes on either side of the balloon. These ropes help spread out the balloon while it is being inflated. If it is windy more people will be needed to hold the balloon in place.

Once all the lines are secured, the cold inflation can begin. A huge gasoline-powered fan is wheeled near the mouth of the balloon. With arms stretched over his head, the pilot or crew member holds the balloon open for inflation. The fan is started. Soon a steady stream of air is pushed into the mouth of the balloon.

The fabric flutters and stirs. Within minutes the balloon begins to take shape. It looks like a giant whale sleeping on the beach. Stepping inside the balloon, the pilot checks the fabric for holes or tears. He also tests the rip panel at the crown of the balloon and the maneuvering vent. Before he leaves the balloon he gathers up the ripcord, the vent cord, and the pyrometer cord and carries them outside. Then he attaches each one to its proper place on the basket.

The air bag is almost two-thirds full. It is time to use the burner. The end of the burner is aimed at the middle of the balloon's opening. Long hot blasts are used to warm the air inside the balloon. As the air warms up and expands the balloon grows larger and larger. The crew must hold the ropes very tight. If the balloon is allowed to "stand up" too soon it could roll over or twist to the side.

The pilot continues to shoot hot flames into the balloon. As the balloon fills out, the pilot orders the crew to "ease off" on their lines. Without letting go completely, the crew members relax their grip. Soon the balloon will be ready to rise off the ground. After a few more blasts from the burner, the pilot shouts, "Let her up!" Everyone drops their ropes at once and the big colorful balloon pops up into position. The crew cheers. Their balloon is standing.

The basket is now seated correctly on its base. The pilot is in the basket in case the balloon should fly away. The balloon is kept in place by the crew. They lean on the edge of the basket with two hands. The pilot checks his instruments. Everything seems to be working. He is ready for his passengers to climb aboard. The passengers are helped into the basket.

The rest of the ground crew has loaded the big

fan and extra tanks of fuel into the chase vehicle. Everyone is ready to go.

The pilot turns the valve of the burner and the blue-ish flames shoot up. The balloon wants to fly. The people holding the basket have to press down with all their weight to keep the balloon on the ground.

"Hands off," calls the pilot and immediately the balloon takes to the sky. "Goodbye," wave the ground crew before piling into the chase vehicle.

"Goodbye," wave the passengers as they float higher and higher into the morning sky. A slight breeze begins to push them gently to the east.

# The Job of the Ground Crew

The ground crew is vital to the operation of any hot air balloon. A pilot needs at least three experienced crew members to launch his balloon. A ground crew of five or six is much better.

Anyone can join a ground crew. At many of the balloon festivals, volunteers from the crowd are asked to help the ground crew hold the lines.

Once the balloon is in the air, the ground crew becomes the chase team. The chase team tries to follow the balloon wherever it goes. A truck, van or station wagon is used as the chase vehicle. Most chase teams have two-way radios to keep in contact with the balloon. Sometimes the wind pushes the balloon out of range or there is a problem with the radio. For this reason, it is important that the chase team keep the balloon in sight.

The chase vehicle is there to help the balloonists if they get into trouble. Balloons can be pushed into trees or power lines by gusts of wind. Changing wind patterns or a sudden storm can also cause problems for the balloon. The chase team must be ready to bring help in case of an emergency.

It is not easy keeping up with a hot air balloon. The balloon floats over fields, hills, rivers, lakes and even mountains. The chase vehicle has to drive around these obstacles. One chase team leader remembers the time his balloon flew across a river.

"We had to drive away from the balloon to find the bridge over the river. By the time we caught up with the balloon it had crossed back over the river to the other side," he laughs. "The people in the balloon could see what was happening but couldn't keep the balloon in one spot. They thought it was pretty funny."

Sometimes the chase team loses sight of their balloon. One team lost their balloon for three hours. A 28 MPH wind carried the balloon away faster than they could follow. The balloon sailed over some hills and eventually made a bumpy landing in the middle of an Indian reservation.

It was January and very cold. The pilot and his two passengers built a small fire to keep themselves warm. Another chase team in the area saw the smoke. They helped the pilot pack up his balloon and gave him a ride to the highway. There they were finally reunited with their own chase team.

"The spirit of friendship among balloonists is incredible," says Dolores Pickens, a passenger on the lost balloon. "If someone is in trouble everyone jumps to the rescue."

Some people think it is more fun bouncing along in the chase vehicle than floating gently through the sky. The chase team wants to be at the landing site when the balloon comes down. They are needed to grab the towlines so that the balloon doesn't bounce or drag along the ground. Once the balloon has landed, the

ground crew will help pack the balloon back into its bag and carry everything back to the truck. Some ground crews make this job into a fun game. To get all the air out of the balloon, several people lie down near the mouth of the balloon. Then they start to roll towards the crown of the balloon. The large rip panel at the crown is open so the air can escape. This is called rolling the air out.

Once most of the air is out, the crew begins to fold and stuff the balloon into it's large storage bag. This takes several pairs of hands. While the balloon is being loaded into the bag, the crew removes any twigs, leaves or dirt which might be stuck to the fabric.

The burner frame and the cables are placed into the same bag before it is sealed shut.

The propane burner and the instruments are carefully packed away before the wicker basket is loaded into the chase vehicle.

With everything stowed away, the job of the ground crew is now complete. It is time to celebrate another successful flight.

# Races, Rallies and Competitions for Hot Air Balloons

The first hot air balloon rally was held at the St. Paul (Minnesota) Winter Carnival in January of 1962. Three balloons took to the sky. In 1988 at the Albuquerque International Balloon Fiesta in New Mexico, a world record 605 hot air balloons were on hand. The Albuquerque Fiesta is the largest in the world. People come from Australia, Japan and Switzerland to take part in this spectacular event. The sport of hot air ballooning continues to grow.

Albuquerque is not the only place you will find hot air balloons. Balloon festivals, rallies and races are held all over the world. The best place to see the sport in action is at a balloon rally. Pilots and crews race for trophies, money, new cars or a new balloon.

In a car race, the first person to drive across the finish line is the winner. Balloon racing is different. The object of a balloon race is how well the pilot can control his balloon. There are several games of skill that test a pilot's know how.

A favorite game is the Hound and Hare. This race is like Follow the Leader. One balloon takes off first. This is the Hare. Then the other balloons, the Hounds, take off. The Hounds try to follow the Hare and land as close to the first balloon as they can.

Two other popular events are the Target Drop and the Key Grab. To win the Target Drop, a pilot must drop a marker on a target from high in the air. The pilot whose marker is the closest wins. At some contests they try to drop a hula hoop over a pole or a golf ball into a hole. The pilot must bring his balloon in as close as he can before he makes his shot.

The Key Grab is one of the most exciting events to watch. Pilots try to fly their balloons very close to a tall pole. On top of the pole is a set of car keys. The pilot who can grab the keys from the top of the pole is the winner. He gets to take home a new car!

If a balloon rally is near a river or lake, you might see balloons playing a game called Splash and Dash. The pilot brings his balloon over the water. Then he lets out a little air until the bottom of the basket just barely touches the water. This is very difficult. Sometimes they let out too much air and the basket hits the water with a big splash. With a blast from the burner, the balloon is pulled out of the water. A good pilot tries to skip across the water like a stone.

One of the most exciting things that happens at a balloon rally is the mass launch. This is when several balloons rise up into the sky at once. Nothing can compare with the gigantic lift-off of over 600 balloons at Albuquerque's Fiesta. Most festivals send anywhere from 12 to 100 balloons up into the air at one time.

A new exhibit at balloon festivals is called Balloon Glow. This event takes place at night. Inflated balloons are held in place by long ropes. When the pilots turn on the burners, the balloons glow like Christmas tree lights.

Balloon rallies are a great place to see a lot of hot air balloons at one time. The people are very friendly and are happy to tell you all about their balloons. Yearly festivals and rallies are held all over the country. Here is a partial list of some of the bigger events. These festivals take place around the same time every year.

**The National Championships** are held at Baton Rouge, Louisiana in early August.

**The National Balloon Classic** is held at Indianola, Iowa in early August.

**The Albuquerque International Balloon Fiesta** is held in Albuquerque, New Mexico the first full weekend in October.

**The International Balloon Championships** are held in Battle Creek, Michigan during the month of June.

**The Freedom Weekend Aloft** is held in Greensville, South Carolina on the Fourth of July weekend.

**The Adirondack Balloon Festival** is held in Glens Falls, New York during the month of September.

**The Great Reno Balloon Race** is held in Reno, Nevada the weekend after Labor Day.

**The Thunderbird Balloon Classic** is held in Glendale, Arizona in mid-November.

# How to Get Involved in Hot Air Ballooning

There are more hot air balloons in the United States than in any other country. There are over 5,000 registered pilots flying in America. Almost every state has a hot air ballooning association or club. These groups often sponsor local balloon rallies and events.

The easiest way to get into ballooning is to join a local club. The club will put you to work on the ground crew. Being a member of the ground crew is the best way to learn about ballooning. You will learn about the different parts of the balloon and how they work. You will be part of the team that inflates and deflates the balloon. You may even join the chase team and follow the balloon wherever it leads. Sometimes, crew members ride in the balloon.

After working on a ground crew, some people decide they want to become an aeronaut (balloon pilot). It is easier to earn a balloon pilot's license than an airplane pilot's license. There are three kinds of balloon licenses: student, private and commercial.

A student pilot must be at least 14 years old. The young pilot starts out by working on the ground crew. A student pilot must always fly under the watchful eye of an instructor.

During the first few flights, the balloon will not fly free. It will be held in place with several long ropes. This gives the student a chance to learn how to fly without getting into trouble. The student pilot can practice takeoffs and landing without worrying where the wind is taking him.

The instructor and student will fly together many times. The student will learn how to handle the balloon under a variety of conditions. When the instructor feels he is ready, he will send the student up on a solo flight. This is the first time the student pilot will fly alone.

Scott Vesely of New Mexico had his student license at age 14. He still remembers the first time he went up in a balloon. "I was 12 years old and I was scared to death. My knees were shaking. But I loved it. It's a totally different world in the air. It's nothing like it is on the ground." A student pilot cannot take passengers up in his balloon. He will need a private pilot's license to take his friends for a ride. After training as a student pilot for two years, Scott went on to earn his private license when he was 16 years old.

To earn a private license, the pilot must be at least 16 years old and pass several tests. The written test asks questions about how a balloon works. The pilot must know how to read charts and maps. He must also understand weather patterns and how they can affect his balloon. Besides the written test, the pilot must have at least ten hours of flying time in a balloon. The pilot must prove that he can handle his balloon safely.

A pilot with a private ballooning license can take his friends for a ride or fly alone. If he wants to charge people money to ride in his balloon or give flying lessons, he will need a commercial license. This is the most difficult license to get. The pilot must pass several different tests to receive his commercial license.

Serious balloonists join the Balloon Federation of America, known as the BFA. This organization sponsors balloon events across the country. Members of BFA can find out where local events are taking place by reading "Skyline", a monthly newsletter put out by their club. To find out about joining the BFA, write: Balloon Federation of America, P.O. Box 400, Indianola, Iowa, 50125.

Hot air ballooning is a colorful, exciting sport the entire family can enjoy. Like a huge fire-breathing dragon, you will be able to sail over tree tops or soar with the birds. Whether you watch from below or fly in the sky, it is an experience you will never forget.

# Glossary

**Alitmeter:** An instrument used to determine the altitude of the balloon.

**Pyrometer:** An instrument used to determine the heat of the gases that keep the balloon in the air.

**Tethers:** A rope attached to the balloon and to the ground to keep the balloon a little above the ground.

**Variometer:** An instrument used to check the magnetic field of the earth.